CW00957241

How to Climb™ Series

Knots for Climbers

Second Edition

Craig Luebben

FALCONGUIDES ®

GUILFORD, CONNECTICUT
HELENA, MONTANA
AN IMPRINT OF THE GLOBE PEQUOT PRESS

FALCONGUIDES®

Copyright © 2002 Morris Book Publishing, LLC
A previous edition of this book was published by Falcon Publishing, Inc.
in 1995.

Cover photo: Craig Luebben

Text design: Angela Capone

Illustrations: Steve Dieckhoff

Photo credits: All photos are by Craig Luebben.

Library of Congress Cataloging-in-Publication Data

Luebben, Craig.
   Knots for climbers/Craig Luebben.—2nd ed.
      p. cm.—(A Falcon guide) (How to climb series)
   ISBN 978-0-7627-1218-2
   1. Rock climbing. 2. Rock climbing—Equipment and supplies. 3. Rock
climbing—Safety measures. 4. Knots and splices. I. Title. II. Series.
III. Series: How to climb series

GV200.2.L85 2001
796.52'23—dc21
                                                              2001040909

Printed in the United States of America
Second Edition/Seventh Printing

CONTENTS

Acknowledgments   vi

Introduction   vii

    Climbing Safety   vii

Knots   1

The Twelve Essential Climbing Knots   2

    Tying into the Rope   2

       1. Figure-8 Follow-Through (Flemish Bend) 2

       2. Fisherman's Backup 3

    Tying into the Anchors   4

       3. Figure-8 on a Bight 4

       4. Clove Hitch 5

    Knots for Webbing   6

       5. Water Knot (Ring Bend) 6

       6. Girth Hitch 7

    Tying Cord   8

       7. Double Fisherman's Knot (Grapevine) 8

    Joining Rappel Ropes   9

       8. Square Fisherman's Knot 9

       9. Overhand Knot 10

    Rappel Backup   12

       10. Autoblock 12

    Friction Knot for Ascending a Rope or Escaping the Belay   14

       11. Klemheist Knot 14

    Improvised Belay/Rappel Device   15

       12. Münter Hitch 15

More Useful Climbing Knots   16

Tying into the Rope   16

13. Double Bowline 16

14. Bowline on a Coil 17

15. Butterfly Knot 18

Tying into Anchors   19

16. Overhand Knot on a Bight. 19

17. Equalizing Figure-8 20

Tying Ropes and Cord Together   22

18. Triple Fisherman's Knot 22

19. Figure-8 Fisherman's Knot 23

Knotting Rope Ends for Rappelling   24

20. Stopper Knot 24

Tying Off Protection   25

21. Slip Hitch 25

Friction Knots for Self-Rescue   26

22. Prusik Knot 27

23. Bachman Knot 28

Load-Releasable Knots for Self-Rescue   29

24. Mule Knot 29

25. Münter Mule 30

26. Mariner's Knot 31

Ratcheting Knot for Hauling   32

27. Garda Knot 32

Equipment   33

Ropes   33

Slings and Webbing   38

Carabiners   39

Harnesses   40

*This book is dedicated to my early climbing partner, Newt Wheatley,
who died in an avalanche in 1993.*

ACKNOWLEDGMENTS

Many thanks to Rob Kelman, Tayve Friedman, and Steve Young, who reviewed
the first edition of this book. Artist-carpenter-climber Steve Dieckhoff drew
night and day to create the knot illustrations. As a result, each of these
knots is forever burned into his brain.

Thanks also to the models, Jen Barrientos, Jen Judge, and Cameron Cross.

ABOUT THE AUTHOR

Craig Luebben is an AMGA-certified rock guide. His climbing manual,
Advanced Rock Climbing, coauthored with John Long, won the Mountain
Exposition Award at the 1997 Banff Mountain Book Festival. He is also a
frequent contributor to *Rock & Ice* and *Climbing* magazines.

INTRODUCTION

By itself, a climbing rope is useless. Add a few knots, and suddenly the rope comes to life.

This book covers all the knots you'll ever need for climbing, but it won't teach you how to climb. If you're new to outdoor climbing, it's wise to take several rock climbing courses before venturing out on your own. If you can't afford several, at least do a couple—it's your life we're talking about! Nothing can substitute for the wisdom and experience provided by a professional mountain guide. Hire only American Mountain Guides Association– or International Federation of Mountain Guides Association–certified guides, or those who work for a reputable guide service. For a listing of guides in your area, contact the American Mountain Guides Association (AMGA) at 710 10th Street, Golden, CO 80401; (303) 271-0984; www.amga.com.

Supplement your climbing instruction by reading other titles in the How to Rock Climb series—especially *How to Rock Climb!* and *Climbing Anchors* by John Long, and *Advanced Rock Climbing* by John Long and Craig Luebben. *Mountaineering: Freedom of the Hills* is also a valuable resource, as are *Rock & Ice* and *Climbing* magazines.

The more involved your climbing is, the more knots you'll use. For toproping, the figure-8 tie-in alone may suffice. On multipitch routes the twelve essential knots presented here will handle most situations. The other knots covered are useful, but it's better to dial in the twelve essential knots—so you can tie them in the dark in a rainstorm—than it is to half learn all the knots. Remember, some illustrious climbers have used only four or five knots throughout their entire career.

To learn these knots, get some rope, cord, and webbing and practice tying as you read along. Left-handed climbers may prefer tying some of the knots in a mirror image of the illustrations. Practice the knots until you've got them down. Then get out and climb—that's why you're learning these knots!

Climbing Safety

Climbing is exhilarating, challenging, and fun. It requires fitness, balance, and mental control, and allows climbers to reach some of the wildest places on the planet. Climbing is also perilous—climbers must acknowledge and accept this danger. The degree of the risk depends partly on the type of climbing. Bolt-protected sport climbing is safer than alpine rock climbing, and waterfall ice climbing is safer than ascending 8,000-meter peaks. But even toproping can be dangerous if you make a simple mistake. Experience, awareness of hazards, and good judgment are the keys to minimizing risk. Always keep your guard up. Beware of *objective hazards* (those beyond your control, such as natural rockfalls or bad weather) and *subjective hazards* (those resulting from poor judgment or human error). Be conservative—slowly work your way onto more challenging routes, and back off if things don't feel right. Choose safe, knowledgeable partners, because your life is in their hands.

Gravity never sleeps. Every safety detail must be correct when you climb. It's critical that you religiously double-check the entire safety chain before anyone leaves the ground. This includes your harness **B**uckle, the **A**nchor and the rope's attachment to it, the **R**appel/belay device and locking carabiner, and the tie-in **K**not. Just remember **BARK.** You should double-check yourself and your partners, and they should double-check you. I've found unfinished knots and buckles many times during the double-check ritual.

Frequently inspect your soft goods—harness, belay loop, slings, and rope—to be sure they're in good condition. Occasionally inspect your hardware—carabiners, belay/rappel devices, and protection—for wear or notches. Retire gear if you have any doubt about its condition, and consult the manufacturer if you have a question.

Expend the effort to be safe. Getting hurt or killed climbing is bad style.

KNOTS

Knots perform many tasks. They secure us to our ropes and anchors, join webbing and cordage into slings, connect rappel ropes, and enable elaborate self-rescues.

Technically a *knot* forms a loop or noose, fastens two ends of the same cord, or creates a "stopper" in the end of the rope. A *bend* joins two free ends together, and a *hitch* grips a shaft or another rope. Here I use the word *knot* to include all knots, hitches, and bends. The *free end* of the rope is the end that passes and loops around the *standing end* to create a knot. The *load strand* is the strand of rope that's currently bearing weight.

Rope, cordage, and webbing are strongest when loaded in a straight line. When you bend the rope or web to create a knot, it reduces the rope's strength. Some knots are stronger than others—the recommended tie-in knot, the figure-8 follow-through, is one of the strongest. Overall, knot strengths fall into a fairly close range, with the exception of the square knot, which cuts rope strength by more than half.

A finished knot should be neatly dressed, with no extraneous twists, to facilitate easy visual inspection. Knots should always be cinched tight for security.

Knot Strength

Knot	Relative Strength
No knot, tensile pull	100%
Figure-8	70–75%
Double bowline	70–75%
Double fisherman's	65–70%
Water knot	60–70%
Overhand knot	60–65%
Clove hitch	60–65%
Girth hitch	65–70%
Square knot	45%

Tying into the Rope

The tie-in knot is critical—tie it wrong once and it may be the last knot you ever tie. Always double-check your tie-in knots and other parts of the belay chain before leaving the ground.

Knot 1: **Figure-8 Follow-Through (Flemish Bend)**

This is the standard tie-in knot: It's strong, secure, and easy to visually inspect.

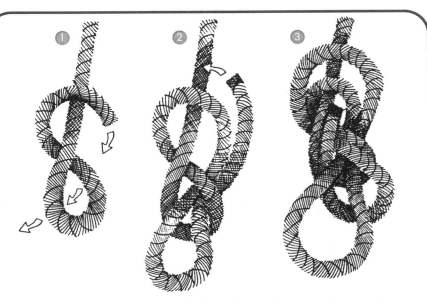

▲ Tie a single 8 in the rope 2 to 3 feet from its end (the exact distance from the end depends on the rope diameter and the backup knot to be used).

▲ Pass the free end of the rope through the harness tie-in point(s), and then retrace the original 8.

▲ Keep the loop inside the knot small. Always secure the figure-8 with a backup knot.

▲ The simplest way to secure the tie-in knot is to pass a 5-inch tail of the rope end one extra time through the figure-8 and cinch it tight. The finishing tail should be around 3 inches long. This extra-pass backup takes less rope and is more compact than a fisherman's backup.

Tie-in knots have a way of untying themselves, especially if the rope is stiff or slick, or if the knot wasn't cinched tight. Some climbers use an overhand knot or half hitch as a backup, but these knots come untied easily. The fisherman's is the most secure backup, because it stays tied once you cinch it tight. It's actually just half of the double fisherman's knot illustrated on page 8.

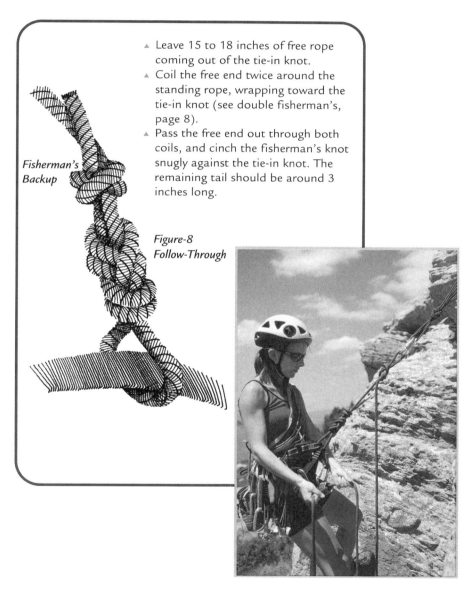

▲ Leave 15 to 18 inches of free rope coming out of the tie-in knot.
▲ Coil the free end twice around the standing rope, wrapping toward the tie-in knot (see double fisherman's, page 8).
▲ Pass the free end out through both coils, and cinch the fisherman's knot snugly against the tie-in knot. The remaining tail should be around 3 inches long.

Fisherman's Backup

Figure-8 Follow-Through

Tying into the Anchors

The figure-8 on a bight is commonly used for tying into anchors, because it's strong and easy to untie after being weighted. The figure-8 is also useful for clipping a climber in midrope, connecting a haul line to the leader (with a locking carabiner), or fastening gear to the haul line. And it can be used to isolate a damaged section of rope (but it won't pass through any carabiners!), or in any other situation where you need a strong loop in the rope.

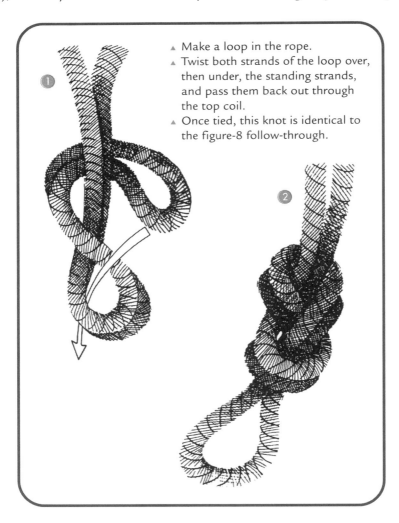

▲ Make a loop in the rope.
▲ Twist both strands of the loop over, then under, the standing strands, and pass them back out through the top coil.
▲ Once tied, this knot is identical to the figure-8 follow-through.

Clove hitches provide quick adjustment and use little rope, but they have a tendency to untie when not loaded, especially when tied in a stiff rope. Be sure they're kept tight at the bottom of the carabiner, away from the gate. A clove hitch is most reliable when tied with a locking carabiner.

The *load strand* of the clove hitch should be situated near the spine of the carabiner. Reversing the clove hitch takes the load away from the carabiner's spine, decreasing carabiner strength up to 30 percent. It's a good idea to tie into the most bombproof anchor with a figure-8 on a bight; clove hitches may be used for the remaining anchors.

▲ Twist two coils into the rope, then pass the second coil in front of the first.

▲ Clip both coils into a carabiner, with the load strand situated near the spine of the carabiner. Cinch the clove hitch tight.

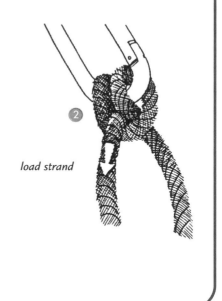

load strand

Knots for Webbing

Knot 5: ▶ Water Knot (Ring Bend)

The water knot is most commonly used for tying webbing into loops. Unfortunately, water knots have a dangerous tendency to "creep" and untie themselves, so the tails must be kept at least 3 inches long, and the knot should be inspected before each use. After you tie a water knot, load the sling with body weight to set the knot. It's possible to fix the tails by taping or lightly sewing them so the knot can't creep. Sewn webbing slings are safer than tied ones because they're stronger and they have no knot to worry about, but knotted slings come in handy for tying around trees or through rock tunnels.

- ▲ Tie a single overhand knot (see step 2, page 11) in one end of the webbing.
- ▲ Match the other end of the webbing to the first end and retrace the overhand knot. Both tails should exit from different sides of the knot, and should be about 3 inches long.

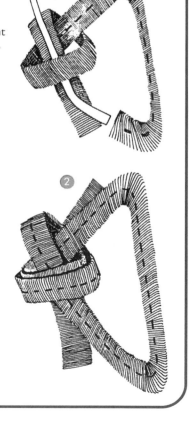

The girth hitch works well for tying off trees, chickenheads, and chockstones. It's also useful for connecting slings together when you're low on carabiners, and for fastening a sling to your harness to create a "cow's tail" for clipping into anchors.

When you're fixing a girth hitch around an object, be sure that the strands passing through the loop run straight. If the strands are forced to bend around the loop (because the loop is too short), it creates a pulley effect, increasing the load on the webbing. If you're tying off a chockstone, this pulley effect might rotate the chockstone out of the crack.

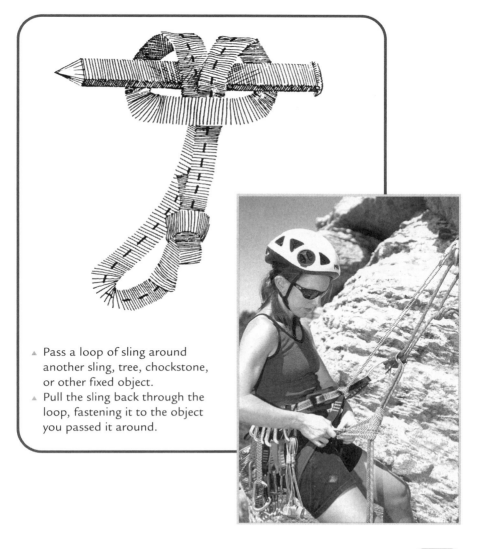

- ▴ Pass a loop of sling around another sling, tree, chockstone, or other fixed object.
- ▴ Pull the sling back through the loop, fastening it to the object you passed it around.

Tying Cord

This knot joins two ropes for rappelling, and fastens accessory cord (such as Perlon, Spectra, or Gemini) into loops for slinging chocks and making cordelette loops. Some climbers also use it for tying webbing slings—it's bulkier than the water knot, but it stays tied better. After rappelling, the double fisherman's can be difficult to untie, especially with skinny or wet ropes, so the square fisherman's knot (see page 9) or overhand knot (page 10) is preferred for joining rappel ropes. For the same reason, it's good to occasionally loosen the double fisherman's knot on your cordelettes, so you can quickly untie the cordelette loop if needed.

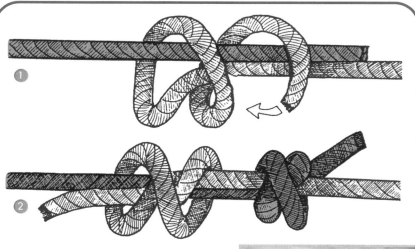

- ▲ Coil the free end of one rope twice around the second rope, and pass it back through the inside of the coils.
- ▲ Repeat the above procedure, this time coiling the second rope around the first, but in the opposite direction so the finished knots are parallel to each other.
- ▲ Pull on all four ends coming out of the knots to cinch them tight. The tails should be about 3 inches long.

Joining Rappel Ropes

Knot 8: ▶ Square Fisherman's Knot

I usually prefer the square fisherman's for joining two rappel ropes, because it's secure and easy to untie—unless I'm worried about getting the rope stuck, in which case the overhand knot is the better choice. The square fisherman's is a square knot secured with two fisherman's backups. *Never use a square knot without the fisherman's backups!* Be careful with new, slick, or stiff ropes, because the fisherman's knots have a way of untying.

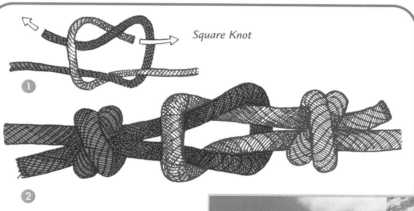

Square Knot

①

②

- ▲ Tie the two ropes together with a square knot. Make sure each strand exits the square knot through the same side of the loop that it entered, so you get a symmetrical shape.
- ▲ Secure the square knot on both sides with a double fisherman's backup (see page 3). This step is crucial!
- ▲ Cinch the square knot tight, then cinch the fisherman's backups tight against the square knot.

The overhand knot is the quickest method for joining two rappel ropes, and it's easy to untie. It has gained widespread acceptance over the past few years, though it still makes me nervous with slick, stiff, or large-diameter ropes. At least one climbing magazine has endorsed it as the best knot for joining rappel ropes, but I would say that if this knot makes you nervous, it's not the best knot. The overhand knot does create the smallest profile, which decreases the chance of getting your ropes stuck. Avoid using the overhand knot on ropes of significantly different diameters, and be very careful with stiff, slick, or large-diameter ropes.

The overhand knot is sufficient for body-weight applications like rappelling, but should never be used where higher forces are possible. For example, for slinging a chock or tying a cordlette into a loop.

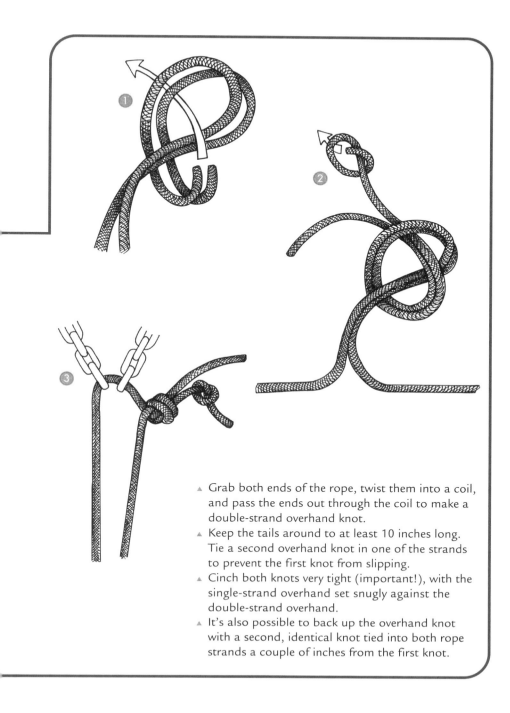

- Grab both ends of the rope, twist them into a coil, and pass the ends out through the coil to make a double-strand overhand knot.
- Keep the tails around to at least 10 inches long. Tie a second overhand knot in one of the strands to prevent the first knot from slipping.
- Cinch both knots very tight (important!), with the single-strand overhand set snugly against the double-strand overhand.
- It's also possible to back up the overhand knot with a second, identical knot tied into both rope strands a couple of inches from the first knot.

Rappel Backup

It's wise to back up your rappel in case anything goes wrong, and so you can easily stop to untangle the rappel ropes. The quickest way is to rig an autoblock on the rappel rope just below the rappel device, and clip it to your leg loop. To rappel, hold the autoblock with your brake hand and keep it loose. If you let go of the autoblock, intentionally or not, the auto-block locks and halts your rappel. To resume rappelling, simply loosen the autoblock. The autoblock also adds friction to your rappel, so you don't burn your hands on steep rappels.

Six-millimeter cord works well for tying the autoblock, but I prefer a ⁵⁄₁₆-inch shoulder-length sling, because it's a standard piece of gear with multiple uses. Spectra webbing works, but nylon creates better friction and has a higher melting temperature. Retire the sling when it becomes worn.

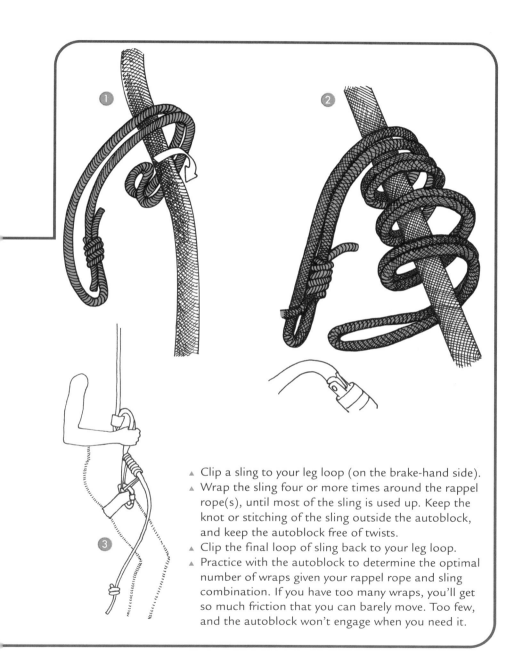

- Clip a sling to your leg loop (on the brake-hand side).
- Wrap the sling four or more times around the rappel rope(s), until most of the sling is used up. Keep the knot or stitching of the sling outside the autoblock, and keep the autoblock free of twists.
- Clip the final loop of sling back to your leg loop.
- Practice with the autoblock to determine the optimal number of wraps given your rappel rope and sling combination. If you have too many wraps, you'll get so much friction that you can barely move. Too few, and the autoblock won't engage when you need it.

Friction Knot for Ascending a Rope or Escaping the Belay

Knot 11: Klemheist Knot

The Klemheist works well for tying off a climber's rope to escape the belay, and for ascending a rope. Once it's unweighted, the Klemheist releases and slides up the rope more easily than the standard prusik. Never trust a life to a single friction knot—always keep them backed up. When escaping the belay, tie the rope off directly to the anchors before removing your belay device from the rope.

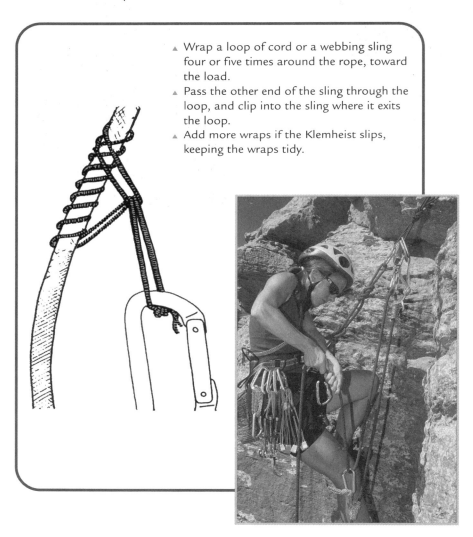

▲ Wrap a loop of cord or a webbing sling four or five times around the rope, toward the load.
▲ Pass the other end of the sling through the loop, and clip into the sling where it exits the loop.
▲ Add more wraps if the Klemheist slips, keeping the wraps tidy.

Improvised Belay/Rappel Device

Knot 12: Münter Hitch

The Münter hitch is a great backup system for belaying and rappelling if you drop your device—every climber should know how to rig it. The Münter works best in large, pear-shaped carabiners, because the hitch must invert through the carabiner when switching from taking in to feeding out rope, or vice versa. Use the Münter hitch only with a locking carabiner, or with two carabiners, gates opposed. To rappel with two ropes, rig the Münter on both strands of rope. When belaying a leader, set the load strand next to the carabiner's spine to get maximum strength from the carabiner. The one bummer is that Münter hitches kink the rope.

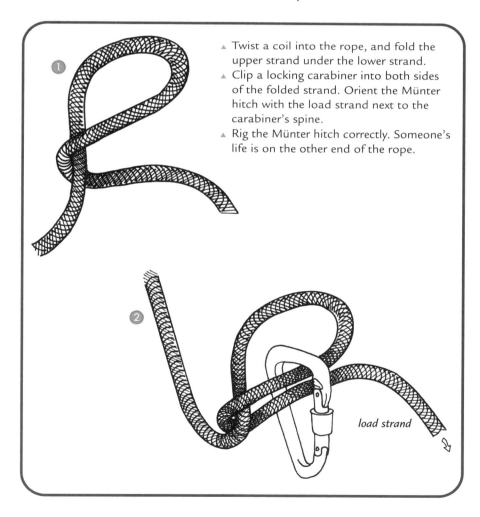

▲ Twist a coil into the rope, and fold the upper strand under the lower strand.

▲ Clip a locking carabiner into both sides of the folded strand. Orient the Münter hitch with the load strand next to the carabiner's spine.

▲ Rig the Münter hitch correctly. Someone's life is on the other end of the rope.

load strand

Tying into the Rope

Knot 13: Double Bowline

The double bowline is great for securing ropes around trees and other features. Some sport climbers use the double bowline for tying into the rope because it has a smaller profile than the figure-8, and it unties easily after being weighted. Unfortunately, because it does untie so easily, the double bowline used as a tie-in knot has resulted in several injuries and deaths. A secure backup knot is essential.

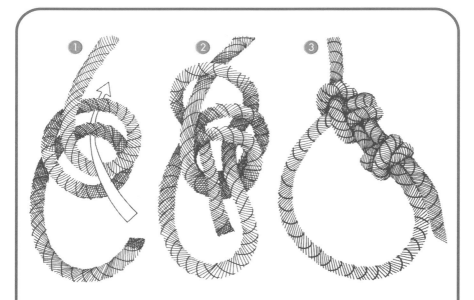

▲ Twist two coils into the rope, with the free end coming out from the bottom of the coils.

▲ Pass the free end around the harness tie-in point (or tree), down through the coils, up around the standing strand of rope, then back down and out through the coils.

▲ Tie a fisherman's backup (see page 3) inside the loop created.

▲ Be sure to tie this knot as shown in the illustration. A number of slight variations exist, but they don't hold much weight.

In the days before climbers had harnesses, they simply lashed themselves to the rope with a bowline on a coil. Thankfully, most modern climbers will never need to use the bowline on a coil, but it could come in handy in an emergency situation if you or the person you're rescuing is without a harness.

The severe rib compression caused by this system can be suffocating if you have to hang on the rope too long. The bowline on a coil can be improved by incorporating webbing leg loops, but climbing harnesses are much safer and more comfortable.

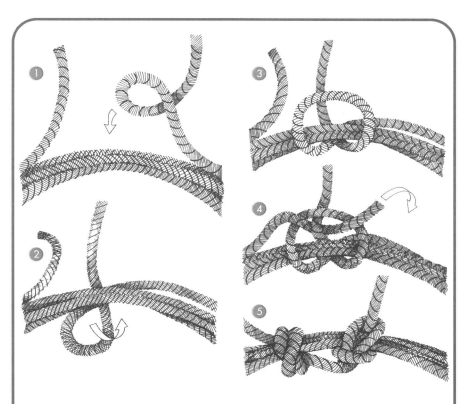

▲ Pass the rope four times around the small part of your waist.

▲ Twist a coil into the rope, with the standing end below the twist.

▲ Pass the coil under the four wraps on your waist and fold it back toward the standing end.

▲ Pass the free end into the coil, around the standing end, and back out through the coil. Cinch all slack out of the knot.

▲ Tie a fisherman's backup (see page 3) around the four waist wraps to secure the bowline.

The butterfly knot is commonly used in glacier travel for tying in the middle climber(s) when traveling three or more to a rope. Its symmetrical shape creates a nice loop for the middle climber to clip into, preferably with two carabiners, including one that locks. The butterfly is also useful for isolating a damaged section of rope.

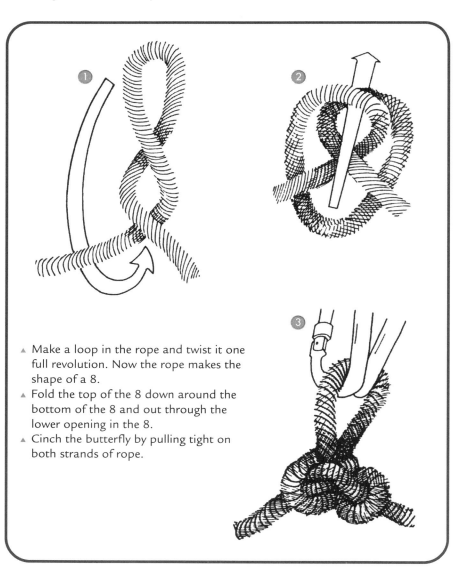

- Make a loop in the rope and twist it one full revolution. Now the rope makes the shape of a 8.
- Fold the top of the 8 down around the bottom of the 8 and out through the lower opening in the 8.
- Cinch the butterfly by pulling tight on both strands of rope.

Tying into Anchors

Knot 16: Overhand Knot on a Bight

The overhand knot is fast and easy to tie for the occasional quick anchor, or for creating a noncritical loop in the rope. Still, the figure-8 is stronger, easier to untie after being weighted, and nearly as fast.

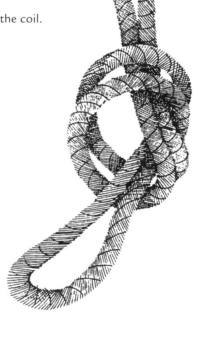

▲ Form a loop with two strands of rope. Twist the loop around itself, forming a coil.
▲ Pass the loop out through the coil.

Equalizing your anchors, so they share the load equally, maximizes the strength of the anchor system. Climbers normally use slings or a cordelette to equalize the load (see *How to Rock Climb* or *Climbing Anchors*), but you can also use the climbing rope, which minimizes the amount of gear required at the belay. While a carefully adjusted string of clove hitches (see page 5) will equalize the anchors somewhat, an equalizing figure-8 spreads the load equally.

Avoid using the equalizing figure-8 if the anchors are far apart, or if they're not bomber, to avoid having the rope run against itself should an anchor pull out. Also, don't use the equalizing figure-8 if the leader is going to need every inch of rope to reach the next belay.

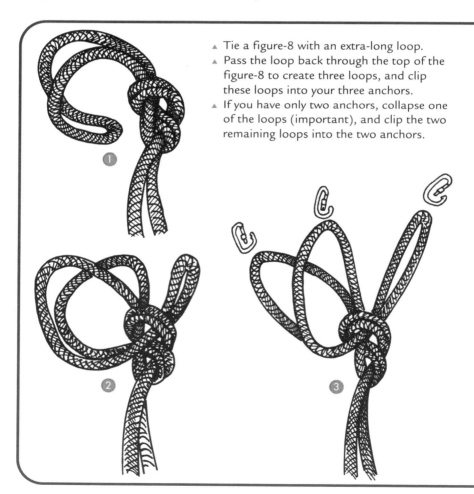

▲ Tie a figure-8 with an extra-long loop.
▲ Pass the loop back through the top of the figure-8 to create three loops, and clip these loops into your three anchors.
▲ If you have only two anchors, collapse one of the loops (important), and clip the two remaining loops into the two anchors.

One version of the equalizing figure-8 incorporates a carabiner to avoid the possibility of nylon running across nylon if an anchor fails. The carabiner also allows you to create any multiple of loops for equalizing the load on several anchors, though this may tie up a lot of climbing rope.

- ▴ Tie a figure-8 on a bight (see page 4) with a large loop, and clip a locking carabiner into the top of the knot.
- ▴ Clip the large loop once through the locking carabiner to create two loops, and clip these loops separately into the two anchors you wish to equalize.
- ▴ For each additional anchor, clip the rope back through the locking carabiner and the new anchor.

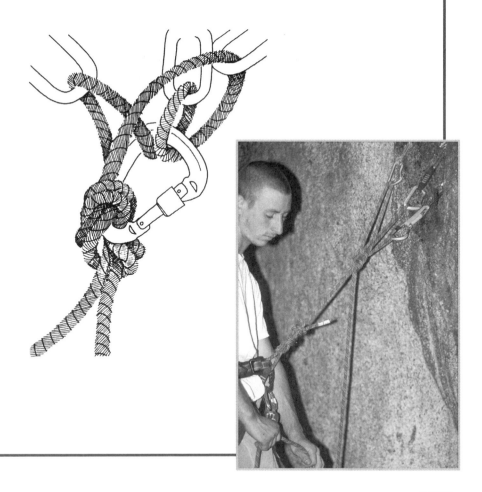

Tying Ropes and Cord Together

Knot 18: Triple Fisherman's Knot

A triple fisherman's knot is recommended for tying Spectra cord, because Spectra is more slippery than other accessory cord materials.

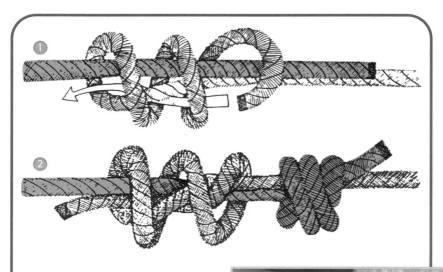

▲ Tie this the same as the double fisherman's (see page 8), but coil the cord ends three times around each other.

Knot 19: Figure-8 Fisherman's Knot

The figure-8 fisherman's is completely secure, so it's great for joining two topropes. It's also good for joining rappel ropes, though the large profile does increase the chance of getting the rope stuck.

- Secure the two ropes together with a figure-8 knot, leaving 15 to 18 inches of tail on both ends. Make sure the ends exit through different sides of the figure-8.
- Tie a fisherman's backup (see page 3) on each side of the figure-8.

Knotting Rope Ends for Rappelling

Knot 20: Stopper Knot

It's important to tie a stopper knot in both ends of the rappel rope(s) before you toss them down, so that you can't accidentally rappel off the ends of the rope. This is especially crucial during bad weather, if it's dark, or if you're not very experienced. The stopper knot does increase the possibility of getting the rope stuck, particularly if it's windy and the rope is blowing sideways, or if the rock is textured with rope-snagging features. A separate overhand knot (see page 10) or figure-8 on a bight knot (page 4) in each rope end also works well. Some people tie both rope ends together with an overhand or figure-8 knot, but this prevents kinks from untwisting at the end of the rope, resulting in tangled ropes.

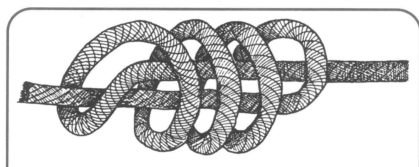

▲ The stopper knot is similar to the double fisherman's knot (see page 8). Coil the rope three or four times around itself and pass the end out through the coils.

▲ Pull both ends to cinch the knot tight. Make sure the tail is at least 3 inches long.

▲ Tie a second stopper knot in the other end of the rappel rope(s).

Tying Off Protection

The slip hitch maintains a "bite" on natural anchors such as chickenheads and pitons that aren't fully driven. Because the slip hitch "locks" onto the chickenhead or piton, it's more secure than a girth hitch.

Tying off a piton that is not fully driven, rather than clipping the eye, reduces the leverage thereby increasing the piton's strength.

▲ Twist a coil into the rope, and pull a loop through this coil.

▲ Set the sling around the chickenhead or piton and cinch the loop tight to secure the sling.

Friction Knots for Self-Rescue

Self-rescue means taking responsibility and dealing with your own problems. Climbers who routinely climb multipitch routes should be proficient in self-rescue techniques. See *Self-Rescue* or *Advanced Rock Climbing*, also in the How to Rock Climb series, for step-by-step instructions in self-rescue techniques, and hire a guide to teach you.

Friction knots lock on the rope when weighted but can be slid when unweighted, so they're fundamental to many self-rescue techniques, including ascending ropes, backing up rappels, creating a ratchet for hauling, and transferring an injured climber's weight to the anchors so you can escape the belay.

The cord used in the friction knot must be significantly smaller in diameter than the rope it grabs. Five- to 6-millimeter-diameter cord works well on 10-millimeter or larger single ropes, or on double strands of thinner ropes. You can also use $\frac{9}{16}$- or $\frac{11}{16}$-inch webbing for friction knots—nylon web works best, but Spectra can also work.

Friction knots grip great on well-used ropes, but sometimes not so well on new, slippery ropes. The more wraps you make around the ropes, the more friction you get. The cord or webbing used for friction knots can burn through if the knot slips down the rope—be sure to have enough wraps, and always keep the wraps tidy and untwisted.

Primarily used for ascending ropes and backing up rappels, the prusik is often difficult to break free and slide after it locks onto the rope. The trick is to loosen the "tongue," or center loop, before attempting to slide it. Because the prusik bites so well, it's good to know in case other friction knots slip (for example on a new, slippery, or skinny rope).

An old-school technique uses the prusik as a rappel backup. The prusik is fastened on the rappel rope(s) just above the rappel device, and connected to a harness tie-in point—NEVER just a leg loop. It's critical that the prusik sling not be so long that it could lock up beyond your reach, leaving you stranded midrappel. The autoblock system described on page 12 is far superior for backing up a rappel.

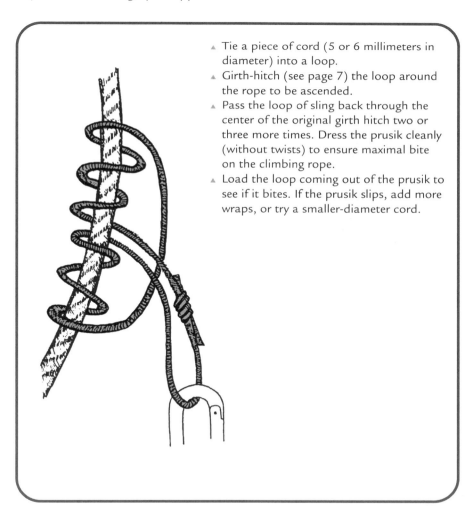

▲ Tie a piece of cord (5 or 6 millimeters in diameter) into a loop.

▲ Girth-hitch (see page 7) the loop around the rope to be ascended.

▲ Pass the loop of sling back through the center of the original girth hitch two or three more times. Dress the prusik cleanly (without twists) to ensure maximal bite on the climbing rope.

▲ Load the loop coming out of the prusik to see if it bites. If the prusik slips, add more wraps, or try a smaller-diameter cord.

The Bachman knot is the best knot for ascending a rope, and it can be tied with cord or webbing. It uses a carabiner as a handle, so it slides up the rope easily after being weighted. You can also use the Bachman with a pulley to create a ratchet for hauling (of course, a Jumar works better for this). The Bachman also can back up a Garda knot (see page 32) in an improvised hauling situation. Weight the Bachman sling rather than the carabiner, or the Bachman will slide down the rope.

▲ Clip a carabiner into a sling or loop of cord.
▲ Wrap the sling or cord about four times around the rope and through the carabiner, keeping the wraps free of twists.
▲ Weight the loop exiting the carabiner. If the Bachman slips when weighted, add more wraps. If it still won't grab, try a smaller-diameter cord, or use a prusik for greater friction.

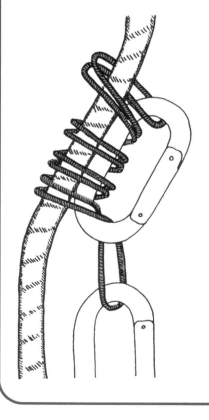

Load-Releasable Knots for Self-Rescue

In many self-rescue situations you have to transfer a climber's weight from one system to another. Using a load-releasable knot—one that can be untied with the climber's weight hanging on it—saves a lot of trouble. Procedures for using the load-releasable knots are covered in *Advanced Rock Climbing* and *Self-Rescue*.

Knot 24: ▶ Mule Knot

The mule knot is a load-releasable knot that allows you to tie off an injured climber to your belay device so you can free your hands to perform a belay escape. You can also use the mule knot to tie off a hanging climber so you don't have to hold his or her weight. And you can tie yourself off with a mule knot when rappelling. It's crucial to back up the mule knot with an overhand or grapevine for security.

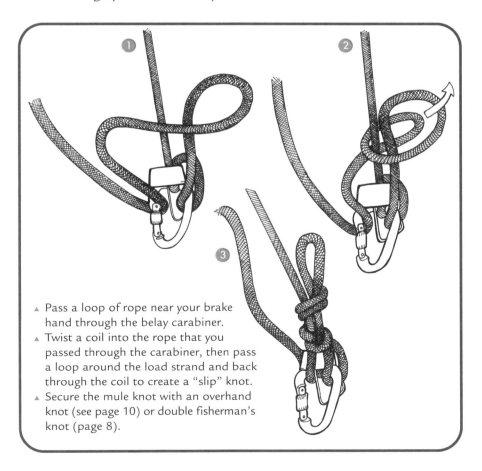

▲ Pass a loop of rope near your brake hand through the belay carabiner.
▲ Twist a coil into the rope that you passed through the carabiner, then pass a loop around the load strand and back through the coil to create a "slip" knot.
▲ Secure the mule knot with an overhand knot (see page 10) or double fisherman's knot (page 8).

A Münter mule is load-releasable, so it works well for temporarily tying an injured climber off to the anchors. The Münter mule must be secured with an overhand knot or fisherman's backup.

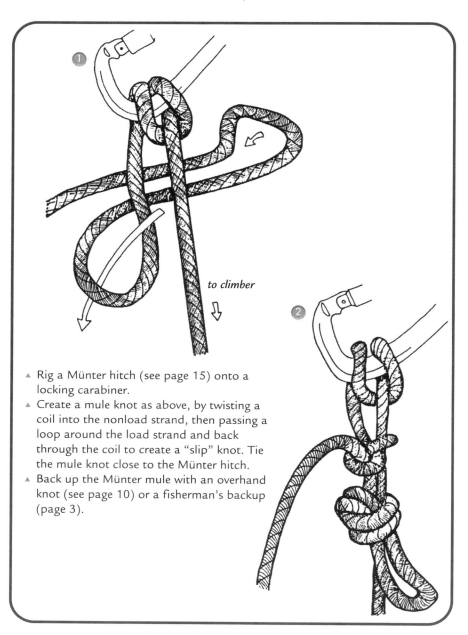

to climber

▲ Rig a Münter hitch (see page 15) onto a locking carabiner.

▲ Create a mule knot as above, by twisting a coil into the nonload strand, then passing a loop around the load strand and back through the coil to create a "slip" knot. Tie the mule knot close to the Münter hitch.

▲ Back up the Münter mule with an overhand knot (see page 10) or a fisherman's backup (page 3).

You can use a webbing sling to transfer the weight of an injured climber from your belay device to the anchors. First attach the sling to the climbing rope with a Klemheist, then fasten the sling to the anchors with a mariner's. The mariner's knot can be released under load, and works best with %₆- to ¹¹⁄₁₆-inch webbing.

Always keep the climber backed up—never trust a life to a single friction knot. Tie the climber off directly to the anchors before freeing the rope from your belay device.

▲ With a double shoulder-length sling, fasten a Klemheist (see page 14) around the rope leading from your belay device to the climber.

▲ Wrap the other end of the sling twice around a carabiner connected to the anchors. If the sling won't reach the anchors, use extra slings or the climbing rope to extend the anchors.

▲ Coil the loop four or more times around the sling, then pass the loop between the two strands of the sling. Tension on the slings holds the mariner's knot tight.

▲ With a carabiner, clip the final webbing loop back to the webbing or anchor carabiner to back up the mariner's knot.

Ratcheting Knot for Hauling

Knot 27: Garda Knot

The Garda ratchets and allows the rope to pass one way only. It can be used with a Z-rig setup for hauling an injured or overwhelmed partner, and it can replace the lower friction knot when ascending a rope. The carabiners used in the Garda should have the same shape. Locking carabiners won't work, because they don't pinch hard enough to secure the rope. It's easiest to rig the Garda with the carabiner gates opening down. It's a good idea to back up a Garda with a Bachman knot (see page 28) fastened onto the load strand and clipped to the anchors.

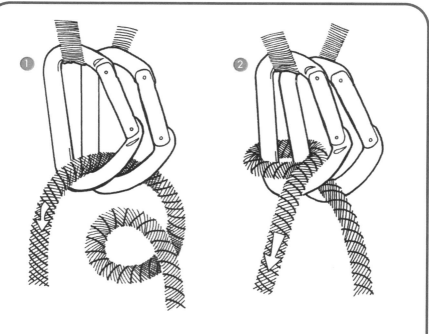

- Clip two carabiners parallel to each other into a sling.
- Pass the rope through both of these carabiners, then back around and through the first one, from the outside to the inside of the carabiner.
- Slide the loop up onto the spines of the two carabiners.
- Be careful to keep the rope from riding up on the gates of the carabiners, lest the Garda come unclipped.

MORE USEFUL CLIMBING KNOTS

Ropes

Climbing ropes are amazingly durable *and* frighteningly fragile. I've used a short section of 9-millimeter diameter Perlon climbing rope to tow cars for sixteen years, yet I've seen brand-new ropes trashed by a sharp edge the first day out. The rope is your lifeline, so treat it with care. Modern climbing ropes range in diameter from 7.8 to 11 millimeters (mm), with breaking strengths of from 3,200 to 5,400 pounds.

Static ropes stretch very little, so they're great for Jumarring (ascending the rope with mechanical devices), while dynamic ropes stretch to absorb the energy of a leader fall. When leading, use only International Union of Alpine Associations (UIAA)–certified dynamic ropes, because they limit the impact force on a falling lead climber and his or her protection. For toproping, rappelling, or hauling, both static and dynamic ropes will work.

Single, Half, and Twin Ropes

Single ropes range in diameter from 9.4 to 11 mm. They're ample for protecting the leader with just one rope. Climbing with a single rope is the lightest and simplest way to go when you don't need two ropes for rappelling. Skinny, lightweight single ropes are good for hard free climbing when every gram counts. But for big walls, working routes (where the leader falls a lot), toproping, or heavy climbers, fat ropes (10.2 mm or bigger) afford a higher safety margin and last longer. Single ropes are marked with a 1 inside a circle.

Half ropes (formerly called double ropes) are used in pairs, and range in diameter from 8.1 to 9.0 mm. They're excellent when the protection doesn't follow a straight line; you can clip one rope on the right and the other on the left to prevent sharp bends that cause rope drag. In addition, with two ropes you have a backup in case you kick one with a crampon or cut it over an edge. Half ropes work well for ice climbing because they lessen the impact force on your protection (provided only one of them is clipped into the piece you're falling on). Of course, less impact comes at the cost of increased rope stretch, which means you're more likely to hit that ledge below. Half ropes are marked with a ½.

The thinnest ropes, 7.8 to 8.5 mm, serve as twin ropes. Because twin ropes are so thin, you should clip them both into every piece of lead protection. This gives them less utility than half ropes, because you can't route them separately to fight rope drag. Twin ropes do work well in alpine situations, because they shave a few ounces and you always have two cords for rappelling. Twin ropes are marked with an infinity symbol in a circle.

Length

Over the last twenty years, climbers have been using increasingly longer ropes. The standard rope length used to be 45 meters; then it grew to 50 meters. Now many climbers use 55-, 60-, and even 70-meter ropes. The most common lengths are 50 meters (165 feet) and 60 meters (198 feet). A longer rope means more to coil, carry, and manage, but the extra utility is often worth it. In some cragging areas, a longer rope might allow you to lower, rappel, or toprope with a single cord, so you can leave the second rope at home. On long routes you can string pitches together to minimize the number of belays. This is great for a competent team, but it's not good for a struggling partner to be 200 feet below you. With two long cords, you can sometimes bypass one rappel station and reach the next. If the rope gets stuck two pitches above, though, you'll regret it.

Dry Ropes

On a wet ice pitch or in a rainstorm, a standard rope can gain several times its weight in water. A wet rope isn't as strong as a dry rope, and if it freezes you end up with a stiff, unusable cable. Because of this, ice climbers and alpinists prefer dry-coated ropes, which repel water—at least when they're new. A dry coating also makes a rope slicker, decreasing rope drag on long rock pitches and possibly helping the sheath last longer. Unfortunately, the dry coating will scrape off after a few dozen rock pitches, so some ice climbers save a pair of dry ropes just for ice climbing. You can re-treat worn ropes with a spray-on coating.

Fall Factor

The greatest demand on a rope is catching a falling leader. During a fall your body gains energy as gravity pulls you toward earth. To stop your fall, the climbing rope acts like a spring, stretching to absorb energy and limit the impact force. Energy is also absorbed by tightening of the tie-in knot, friction in the system, and movement of the belayer. If you hit a ledge or the ground, your body, unfortunately, absorbs the energy of the fall.

The *fall factor* is defined as the length of the fall divided by the amount of rope between the leader and belayer. It strongly influences the amount of impact force generated. A factor-two fall generates the highest force, and occurs if the leader falls before placing protection and is caught directly on the belay anchors. Contrary to intuition, all falls with the same fall factor create the same-impact force, regardless of their length; a 10-foot fall with 5 feet of rope out will (theoretically) produce the same force as a 100-foot fall on 50 feet of rope, because both are factor-two falls. In the shorter fall, less rope is available to absorb energy.

What does all of this mean? When you lead you should place solid protection immediately after leaving the belay, and protect regularly as you lead up the pitch, to decrease the potential fall factor and protect the anchors from a large impact. It also means you need bomber belay anchors.

UIAA Rope Testing

The UIAA tests and certifies dynamic ropes for their fitness to catch leader falls. To ensure adequate strength and impact absorption of a single rope, inspectors drop an 80-kilogram mass (176 pounds) 5 meters on a 2.8-meter section of rope, creating a severe factor-1.8 fall. The ropes must survive at least five test falls, and generate less than 2,640 pounds of impact force on the "climber" during the first drop. A 55-kilogram test mass is used for half ropes, and the impact force must be below 1,760 pounds. Most ropes on the market actually test out well below the designated impact force limits.

The factor-1.8 fall, coupled with the unabsorbing anchor and rigid test weight, makes the UIAA drop test severe. Because the test falls are more punishing than most real-life falls, you don't have to retire a UIAA 9-fall rope after nine routine sport climbing whips. But you should consider retiring it after a few hard falls close to the belay—if you're still climbing.

Rope Care

Climbing ropes are built with kernmantle construction. Braided strands of Perlon form the rope's core, providing strength and shock absorption, while a woven nylon sheath protects the core. Since the core is hidden and cannot be visibly inspected for damage, climbers must pamper their ropes. The golden rules are: Never step on a climbing rope, avoid loading the rope over sharp or rough edges, and avoid chemical contamination of the rope. Stepping on a rope may damage its core strands and grind dirt into its fibers, which further damages the core over time. If you do step on a rope, you probably don't need to retire it, but avoid this as much as possible.

It's also good to keep your rope out of the dirt. A *rope tarp* keeps your rope out of the dirt when you're sport climbing or craggin'. It also allows you to move from climb to climb without coiling your rope—just stack it on the tarp, roll it up, and move to the next route. *Rope bags* provide good protection for storing and transporting climbing ropes, and a *rope cleaner* will remove dirt.

Ropes are also susceptible to damage from ultraviolet radiation (the sun), prolonged exposure to elevated temperatures, chemicals, petroleum products, solvents, and more. For this reason ropes should be stored in a cool, clean, shaded, and dry place. Many people say climbing ropes never break. Tell that to this guy: Recently, a large climber was being lowered. Just before he reached the ground, the rope broke. He fell to the ground, but luckily escaped serious injury. Analysis of the rope showed traces of battery acid, probably picked up in the rat-infested trunk of a vagabond climber. Good thing he wasn't 80 feet off the deck. Track your rope's history, and don't loan it out.

When fixing lines, use static rope whenever possible, because it doesn't stretch and saw over edges as you ascend the way a bouncy lead cord does.

Ropes kink, cluttering your rope management and wasting time. You can minimize kinking by unwinding new, factory-coiled ropes as if you're rolling them off a spool, rather than flaking them out. Also, avoid figure-8 rappel devices, Münter hitches, and the mountaineer's coil to keep your ropes from kinking. To remove kinks, work them out through the end of the rope, or hang the rope down a cliff and let the kinks twist out.

When to retire a rope? It's certainly time when a hole wears through the sheath and exposes the core, or if you take a severe fall. You can test the integrity of a rope's core by pinching the rope between two fingers, then rolling a loop down the length of the rope. If you find flat spots—where the rope doesn't form a loop but instead folds in half—retire it. Ropes used occasionally should be retired from lead climbing after about four years. A rope abused regularly by weekend warriors should be retired after about two years; full-time climbers get about three months to a year out of their ropes.

Lastly, a word on partner care. Always tie into the end of the rope when belaying a leader from the ground, or at least have a knot tied in the end of the rope. This way you can never lower the leader off the end of the rope—a careless mistake that has injured and killed scores of climbers.

Packing a Rope

EQUIPMENT

- Grab both ends of the rope and measure out three complete arm spans. Drop this on the ground for tying the coil together at the end.
- Fold the double strands of rope back and forth across your hand until all the rope is folded. You can also fold the double rope around your neck to save strength.
- Wrap the original three arm spans of rope tightly around the coil about four times, slightly above the coil's midpoint.
- Pass a bight of rope through the hole formed at the top of the coil, then pull the ends through this bight.
- Use the two free ends to tie the rope onto yourself, backpack-style.

Slings and Webbing

Webbing slings, workhorses in the climber's arsenal, are used in many ways for rigging anchor systems and clipping into anchors. Used judiciously by the lead climber, they also reduce rope drag and minimize the "rope wiggle" and sideways pulls that dislodge chocks. Webbing loops also serve as shoulder slings for carrying gear, and they can be fashioned into improvised seat or chest harnesses. Sport climbers need only a handful of quickdraws for clipping bolts, and a couple of shoulder-length slings for clipping the top anchors. Those who climb traditional routes need quickdraws and four to eight shoulder-length slings. A double-length sling or two also comes in handy, especially on longer routes.

Slings can either be tied into a loop with a water knot, or sewn into a loop by a gear manufacturer. Sewn slings are stronger, are more compact, and can't accidentally come untied, while knotted slings can be untied for threading through rock tunnels and around chockstones and trees. It's probably best to have some of each for longer routes.

Webbing for climbing has traditionally been manufactured from nylon. It's now also available in Spectra, an amazingly strong fiber. On the downside, Spectra is slick, so it doesn't work as well as nylon for friction knots; it also has a low melting temperature, which makes it susceptible to damage if a nylon rope passes rapidly over it. (Nylon webbing also exhibits this problem, but to a lesser degree.) Webbing is available in a variety of widths. The most common sizes for climbing are listed in the table below, along with their strengths.

Webbing Strength

Webbing type and size	Tensile Strength (pounds)	Loop Strength (sewn)
$\frac{9}{16}$" nylon Super Tape	2,500	4,500
$1\frac{1}{16}$" tubular nylon	4,000	6,800
1" tubular nylon	4,500	6,000–7,400
$\frac{9}{16}$" Spectra webbing		6,500

Carabiners

Climbers today can choose from dozens of models of carabiners. Most come in three basic shapes: oval, D, and asymmetrical D. The D and asymmetrical D provide the highest strength. The UIAA specifies a breaking strength for carabiners of at least 20 kN (4,400 pounds) with the gate closed, and 7 kN (1,540 pounds) with the gate open.

Cross loading and loading over an edge lower the strength of a carabiner; outward loading on the gate is dangerous. If proper carabiner loading can't be facilitated by using slings, use two carabiners with gates opposed. Both carabiner gates should open downward when opposing carabiners. Locking carabiners should be used for connecting yourself to anchors, setting up rappel/belay devices, and sometimes for clipping critical lead protection.

Bent-gate carabiners allow you to slap the rope quickly into the bowed gate, a definite boon on desperate sport routes. They were originally designed for winter climbing, to facilitate easy clipping while wearing gloves. They should be used only on the rope side of a quickdraw, and never for clipping into bolts. Unfortunately, because the rope clips in so easily, it also unclips easily, so bent-gate carabiners can be dangerous, particularly if the rope is running across the gate.

Wire-gate carabiners are also easy to clip, and they leave a good amount of clearance inside the carabiner. They also minimize gate flutter—when the gate of a carabiner vibrates open and shut while catching a fall. If the peak impact hits with the gate open, the carabiner has a good chance of breaking.

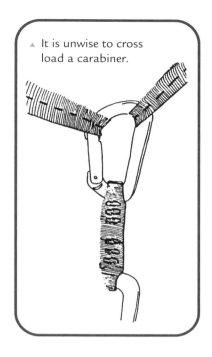

It is unwise to cross load a carabiner.

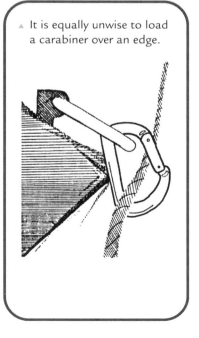

It is equally unwise to load a carabiner over an edge.

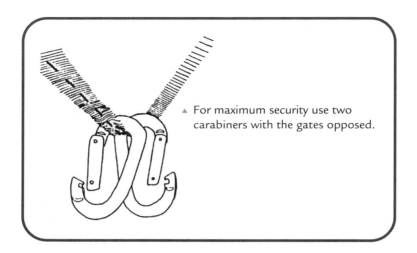

▲ For maximum security use two carabiners with the gates opposed.

Harnesses

The climbing harness connects a climber's rope to his or her body. The harness, rope, and belay device are the only single links in the belay chain—everything else can be backed up. These single links must be in good condition and rigged absolutely right. The harness must fit properly, unable to slide down over the hips, with the leg loops almost snug but not restrictive. Most harnesses fasten around the climber's waist with a buckle for convenience and easy adjustment. The buckle *must be double-passed* to secure the harness (instructions should be sewn onto the harness). Most good harnesses have a sewn webbing belay loop for connecting a belay or rappel setup to the harness. The belay loop must be in good shape, since you rely completely upon it. Other useful features include sufficient padding, gear racking loops, and a solid haul loop on the back. Some children and large people have no hip projections, so it may be necessary for them to use a seat-and-chest harness or a full-body harness. Home-rigged webbing harnesses are uncomfortable, but they can still work in a pinch. Harness should be retired when the webbing becomes worn, or after five or six years.